THE PUSHBUTTON TELEPHONE SONGBOOK

by

MICHAEL SCHEFF

Assisted by
Ralph Martell and
Mary Anne Kasica

PRICE / STERN / SLOAN
Publishers, Inc., Los Angeles

THIRD PRINTING — NOVEMBER 1972

Copyright © 1972 by Michael Scheff
Published by Price/Stern/Sloan Publishers, Inc.
410 North La Cienega Boulevard, Los Angeles, California 90048
Printed in the United States of America. All rights reserved.
Library of Congress Catalog Card Number: 72-877729
ISBN: 0-8431-0258-5

SONG CREDITS

PICTURE CREDITS

HAIL TO THE PUSHBUTTON TELEPHONE

About the only bond people the world over seem to have these days is (1) a desire for peace and (2) a dislike of The Telephone Company.

Apparently aware of their public relations problem, The Phone Company decided to do something about it — something truly worthwhile.

They have provided us with the twentieth century's newest and most unique musical instrument.

Hail to the Pushbutton Telephone!

Our first personal experience with one of these wonders came at a Washington diplomatic party. A number of government people were huddled around a telephone, giving the distinct impression that a major international crisis was in progress. On closer look, it turned out to be an Under-Secretary of something-or-other tapping out *Twinkle, Twinkle Little Star* to a friend at the Justice Department!

Today, the Pushbutton Telephone is everywhere. Millions more are on the way. Eventually all phones will be pushbutton.

And, thanks to The Telephone Company, happy musical messages will be a vital part of our brave new world.

Michael Scheff
Los Angeles

"Can he really play?" a girl whispered. "Heavens, no!" Arthur exclaimed. "He never played a note in his life."

They Laughed When I Sat Down
At the Piano
But When I Started to Play!—

ARTHUR had just played "The Rosary." The room rang with applause. Then to the amazement of all my friends, I strode confidently over to the piano and sat down.

"Jack is up to his old tricks," somebody chuckled. The crowd laughed. They were all certain that I couldn't play a single note.

"Can he really play?" I heard a girl whisper to Arthur.

"Heavens, no!" Arthur exclaimed. "He never played a note in all his life. . . ."

I decided to make the most of the situation. With mock dignity I drew out a silk handkerchief and lightly dusted off the piano keys. Then I rose and gave the revolving piano stool a quarter of a turn. The crowd laughed merrily.

Then I started to play. Instantly a tense silence fell on the guests. I played the first few bars of Liszt's immortal Liebestraume. I heard gasps of amazement. My friends sat breathless—spellbound! I played on.

A Complete Triumph!

As the last notes of the Liebestraume died away, the room resounded with a sudden roar of applause. I found myself surrounded by excited faces. Everybody was exclaiming with delight—plying me with rapid questions. "Jack! Why di . . .

Pick Your . . .

"I have been studying only a short while," I insisted. "I kept it a secret so that I could surprise you folks."

How I Learned to Play Without a Teacher

Then I told them the whole story.

"It seems just a short while ago that I saw an ad of the U. S. School of Music, mentioning a new method of learning to play which only cost a few cents a day! The ad told how a woman had mastered the piano in her spare time at home—and *without a teacher!* The method she used required no laborious scales or exercises. It sounded so convincing that I filled out the coupon requesting the Free Demonstration Lesson.

"It arrived promptly and I started in that very night to study it. I was amazed to see how easy it was to play this new way. I sent for the course and found it was just as easy as A, B, C! Before I knew it I was playing all the pieces I liked best. I could play ballads or classical numbers or jazz, with equal ease! And I never did have any special talent for music!"

Play Any Instrument

You, too, can now learn music—right at home—in half the usual time. You can't go wrong with this simple method which has already shown almost half a million people how to play their favorite instruments by *note.* Forget that old-fashioned idea that you need special "talent." Just read the list of instruments in the panel, decide which one you want to play and the U. S. School will do the rest.

Send for Our Free Booklet and Demonstration Lessons

Thousands of successful students never dreamed they possessed musical ability until it was revealed to them by a remarkable "Musical Ability Test" which we send entirely without cost with our interesting free booklet and Demonstration Lesson.

Sign and send the convenient coupon now. Instruments supplied when needed, cash or credit. U. S. School of Music, 8911 ___ ___ck Bldg., ___ York City.

INSTRUCTIONS

A few words to the wise are in order.

If you just pick up the receiver and immediately begin tapping out *Strangers In The Night,* you might find yourself connected to someone in Nome, Alaska.

So, to play pushbutton phone songs properly, always call up a nearby friend and tap out your songs to him or her. Pressing the buttons on your phone does *not* disconnect you from the person you are talking to! Or, for experimental or demonstration purposes, you can call the tape-recorded time operator and play over her recorded message. We're sure you'll figure it all out very quickly.

Happy playing.

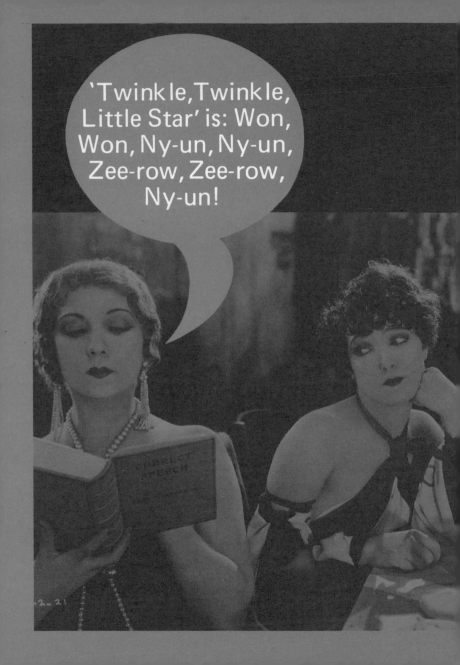

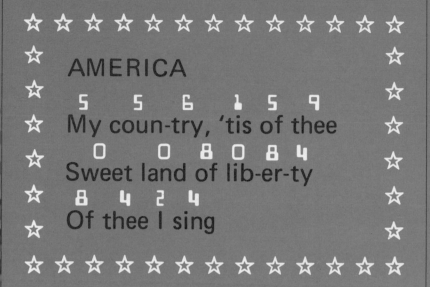

AMERICA

5   5   6   1 5   9

My coun-try, 'tis of thee

0   0   8 0 8 4

Sweet land of lib-er-ty

8   4   2   4

Of thee I sing

TWINKLE, TWINKLE, LITTLE STAR

1   1   9   9

Twin-kle, Twin-kle,

0 0 9

Lit-tle Star

STRANGERS
IN THE NIGHT

4   8   8   4   8

Stran-gers in the night

4   8   6   8   4

Ex-chang-ing glan-ces

HERE COMES THE BRIDE

1   3   3   3

Here comes the bride

1   9   6   6

All dressed in white

IMPORTANT: Push button songs should **only** be played when your phone is connected to someone else's. Otherwise, a long-distance number may be dialed by mistake.

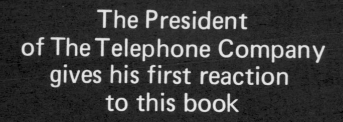

The President
of The Telephone Company
gives his first reaction
to this book

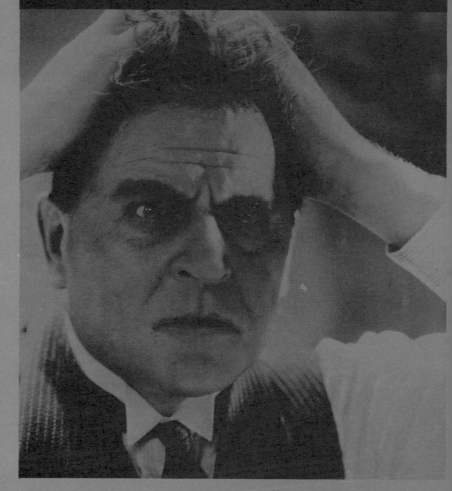

A TISKET A TASKET

6 6 4 8 6 4
A tis-ket a tas-ket

8 6 6 6 9 6 4
A green and yel-low bas-ket

4 6 6 4 4 6 6 4
I wrote a let-ter to my love

8 6 9 6 0 6 4
And on the way I dropped it

8 6 48 6 4
I dropped it I dropped it

8 6 9 6 0 6 4
And on the way I dropped it

8 6 6 4 6 6 4
A lit-tle girl picked it up

8 6 9 6 0 6 4
And put it in her poc-ket

8 6 4 8 6 4
Her poc-ket her poc-ket

HERE WE GO ROUND THE MULBERRY BUSH

4   4   4   2

Here we go round

2   6   6   2   4

the mul-ber-ry bush

4   8   8   8   8

The mul-ber-ry bush

6   2   4   4   4

The mul-ber-ry bush

4   4   4   2

Here we go round

2   6   6   2   4

the mul-ber-ry bush

4   8   8   6   8   4   4

So ear-ly in the morn-ing

LONDON BRIDGE

6 9 6 8 7 8 6
Lon-don Bridge is fall-ing down
1 4 5 7 8 9
Fall-ing down fall-ing down
6 9 6 8 7 8 6
Lon-don Bridge is fall-ing down
8 6 0 4
My fair la-dy

RING AROUND A ROSY

8 8 8 6 0 4
Ring a-round a ros-y
4 8 8 8 6 0 4
A poc-ket full of pos-ies
0 4 0 4 4 0 0 4
Ash-es, ash-es, we all fall down

OLD MACDONALD HAD A FARM

6   6   6   7   8 8 7
Old Mac-Don-ald had a farm

9 9 0 0   4
EE-II-EE-II-OHH!

4 6 6 6 7 8
And on this farm he had

8   7
some chicks

9 9 0 0   4
EE-I-EE-I-OHH!

4 4 4   4   4
With a chick chick here

4 4 4   4   4
And a chick chick there

4 4 4   4 4 4
Here a chick there a chick

4 4 4   4   4   4
Ev-ry-where a chick chick

AU CLAIR DE LA LUNE

4   4   4   0   6   8
Au clair de la lu-ne

4   6   0   0   4
Mon a-mi Pier-rot

4   4   4   0   6   8
Pret-e moi ta plu-me

4   6   0   0   4
Pour e-crire un mot

4   4   4   0   6   8
In the eve-ning moon-light

4   6   0   0   4
My good friend Pier-rot

4   4   4   0   6   8
Lend to me your quill-pen

4   6   0   0   4
Just to write a note

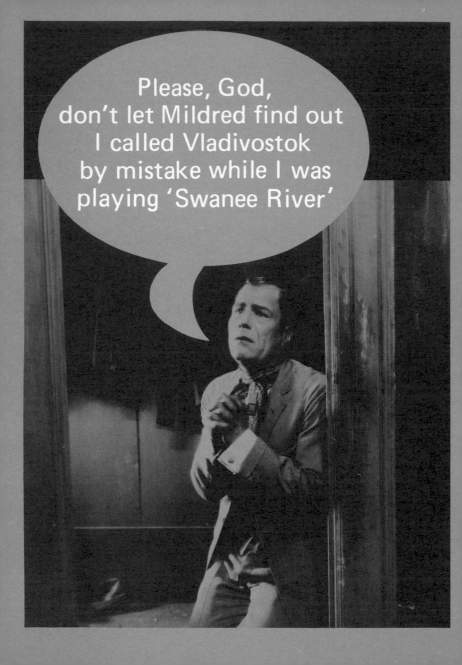

WAY DOWN UPON
THE SWANEE RIVER

3   2   1 3 2
Way down up-on the

1   0 4 5
Swan-ee Riv-er

6 8 4 2
Far far a-way,

3   2 1   3 2
That's where my heart is

1   9 4 5
turn-ing ev-er

6   5   4 2 2   4
That's where the old folks stay

SHAVE AND A HAIRCUT,
TWO BITS

9   4 4 2 1   6   6
Shave and a hair-cut, two bits!

If you keep your nails short
you can play the
pushbutton phone better!

WHEN JOHNNY COMES MARCHING HOME

8   4   4   4   4   8

When John-ny comes march-ing

6 8 6   5   *   5   *

home a-gain Hur-rah! hur-rah!

8   4   4 4   4 8

We'll give him a heart-y

6   8   6   9   #   5   #

wel-come then Hur-rah! hur-rah!

5   #   #   #   5   9

The men will cheer, the boys

9   9   5   6   6   6   4

will shout The lad-ies they will

8   8   8   4   8   #   9

all turn out And we'll all feel

6   8   4   4   4

gay when, John-ny comes

4   0   4

march-ing home

IMPORTANT: Push button songs should **only** be played when your phone is connected to someone else's. Otherwise, a long-distance number may be dialed by mistake.

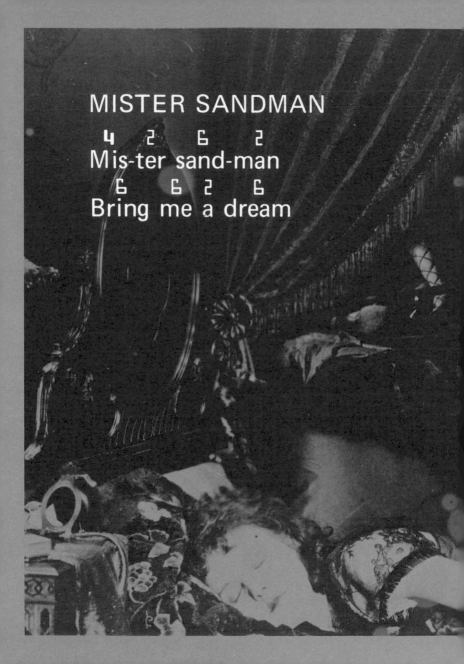

MISTER SANDMAN

4   2   6   2
Mis-ter sand-man
    6   6   2   6
Bring me a dream

That was terrific, Mr. Bell.
Now let's try
'Row, Row, Row Your Boat'
as a round. I'll go first.

ROW, ROW, ROW YOUR BOAT

4   4   4   8   6
Row, row, row your boat

6   2   6   9   #
Gen-tly down the stream

#   # #
Mer-ri-ly

0 0 0
Mer-ri-ly

*   * *
Mer-ri-ly

4 4 4
Mer-ri-ly

6 2 2 1   1
Life is but a dream

MARY HAD A LITTLE LAMB

6 0 4 0 6 6   6

Mar-y had a lit-tle lamb

2 2 2   6 6 6

Lit-tle lamb, lit-tle lamb

6 0 4 0 6 6   6

Mar-y had a lit-tle lamb

6 8   8   6 8 4

Its fleece was white as snow

CALIFORNIA HERE I COME

8 8 8 8   9 8 1

Cal-i-for-nia here I come

3   3   3

Right back where

3 6 3 4

I start-ed from

IMPORTANT: Push button songs should **only** be played when your phone is connected to someone else's. Otherwise, a long-distance number may be dialed by mistake.

COMIN' THROUGH THE RYE

7 7 7 9
When a bod-y
0 7 8 9
Meets a bod-y
1 1 . 5 4 0
Com-in' through the rye

POLLY WOLLY DOODLE

4 2 6 6 4
Oh I went down South
4 2 6 6 4
For to see my gal,
4 2 6 6 6 6
Sing-ing pol-ly wol-ly
0 0 8 8 4
Dood-le all the way

GOOD NIGHT, LADIES

9 7 4 4
Good night, lad-ies,

9 7 2 2
Good night, lad-ies,

9 7 0 0
Good night, lad-ies,

9 6 6 5 5 4
It's time to leave you now.

6 5 4 2 3 3 6
Merr-i-ly we roll a-long,

5 5 8 3 3 6
Roll a-long, roll a-long,

6 5 4 2 3 3 6
Merr-i-ly we roll a-long,

6 5 5 3 2 1
From sea to shi-ning sea

THE OLD GRAY MARE

4   4   4   4
The old gray mare

8   6   6   8   6   8 4
She ain't what she used to be

8   8   4   8   8 4
Ain't what she used to be

6   6   8   6   8 4
Ain't what she used to be

4   4   4   4
The old gray mare

8   6   6   8   6   8 4
She ain't what she used to be

8   8   8   6   8 4
Ma-ny long years a-go

POP GOES THE WEASEL

4 4 8 8 6 8 6 1
All a-round the mul-ber-ry bush

4 4 4 8 6 0 4
The mon-key chased the wea-sel

4 4 4 8
The mon-key thought

8 6 8 6 1
'twas al-l in fun

5 1 6 0 4
Pop goes the wea-sel

I'VE BEEN WORKING
ON THE RAILROAD

7 2 4 5
I've been work-ing

4 2 6 4
on the rail-road

IMPORTANT: Push button songs should **only** be played when your phone is connected to someone else's. Otherwise, a long-distance number may be dialed by mistake.

HAPPY BIRTHDAY

4   4   2   4   #   8

Hap-py birth-day to you

1   1   2   1   9   8

Hap-py birth-day to you

JINGLE BELLS

6   6   6   6   6   6

Jin-gle bells, jin-gle bells

6   #   7   8   6

Jin-gle all the way

9   9   9   9 9   5   5

Oh, what fun it is to ride

5 5 5   7   4   5   6

In a one-horse o-pen sleigh

IMPORTANT: Push button songs should **only** be played when your phone is connected to someone else's. Otherwise, a long-distance number may be dialed by mistake.

OH, SUSANNA

4 8 6 6 9 6 8 7
Oh, I come from Al-a-bam-a

7 8 6 6 0 * 8
With a ban-jo on my knee

4 8 6 6 9 6 8 7
I'm goin' to Louis-i-a-n-a

8 6 6 0 0 4
My true love for to see

9 # 6 6
Oh Su-san-na,

3 2 1 2 3
don't you cry for me

4 8 6 6 9 6 8 7
For I come from Al-a-bam-a

7 8 6 6 0 8 7
With a ban-jo on my knee

Stop! This isn't the guy
who wrote the
Pushbutton Telephone Songbook!!!

COMIN' ROUND
THE MOUNTAIN

4   8
She'll be

8   4
Comin' round the moun-tain

4   8   #
When she comes

THREE BLIND MICE

6   8   4
Three blind mice

6   8   4
Three blind mice

9   5   5   4
See how they run

9   5   5   4
See how they run

I think I got a
thorn in my playing finger

MY OLD KENTUCKY HOME

6　6　6　　4
The sun shines bright

4　2　6　2　6　#　9
In my old Ken-tuck-y home

6　6　2
'Tis sum-mer,

4　4　1　4　8
the peo-ple are gay;

6　6　6　4
The corn-top's ripe

4　2　6　2
And the mead-ow's

6　#　9
in the bloom

4　8　6　6
While the birds make

0　4　6　8　4
Mu-sic all the day

Here's a song for you
to complete yourself.
Easy, isn't it?

YANKEE DOODLE

4 4 2 6 4 6 2

Yan-kee Doo-dle went to town

4 4 2 6 4 1

Rid-ing on a po-ny

4 1 5 6

Stuck a feath-er in his hat

And called it mac-a-ro-ni

FLOW°GENTLY,
SWEET AFTON

1 4 4 6 5 7 7

Flow gen-tly, swe-et Af-ton

IMPORTANT: Push button songs should **only** be played when your phone is connected to someone else's. Otherwise, a long-distance number may be dialed by mistake.

RAMBLING WRECK
FROM GEORGIA TECH.

6 8 4   4   4

I'm a ram-bling wreck

  8   6 6 6

From Geor-gia Tech

  8 4 8 6 8 4 0 4

And a hell of an en-gin-eer

LAZY MARY

4 4 4 4 0 6 0 4

La-zy Mar-y, will you get up

 4 2 2 2 6 8 1 1

Will you get up, will you get up

4 4 4 4 0 6 0 4

La-zy Mar-y, will you get up

 4 5 5 6 8 4

Will you get up to-day

IMPORTANT: Push button songs should **only** be played when your phone is connected to someone else's. Otherwise, a long-distance number may be dialed by mistake.

THE CAISSONS
GO ROLLING ALONG

6 4 3

Ov-er hill,

0 4 3

Ov-er dale,

6 4 3 9 6 7 6

We will hit the dus-ty trail,

1 5 6 2

And those cai-ssons

1 6 5 1 4

Go rol-ling a-long

THE FARMER IN THE DELL

4   4   4   4   4   4

The far-mer in the dell

5   6   6   6   6   6

The far-mer in the dell

\#   \#   9   \#   8   4

Heigh-ho the der-ry-o

4   6   6   8   8   4

The far-mer in the dell

FRERE JACQUES

4   2   6   4   4   2   6   4

Fre-re Jac-ques   Fre-re Jac-ques

6   9   \#   6   9   \#

Dor-mez-vous?   Dor-mez-vous?

IMPORTANT: Push button songs should **only** be played when your phone is connected to someone else's. Otherwise, a long-distance number may be dialed by mistake.

AULD LANG SYNE

8   4   4   4   6

Should auld ac-quain-tance

8   4   8

be for-got

9   1   4   3   9   #

In days of auld lang syne

IMPORTANT: Push button songs should **only** be played when your phone is connected to someone else's. Otherwise, a long-distance number may be dialed by mistake.

This book is published by

PRICE/STERN/SLOAN
Publishers, Inc.

whose other splendid titles include such literary classics as:

You Were Born On A Rotten Day
The China/Russia Papers
The Successful Businessman's Guide
How To Tell If Your Husband Is Cheating On You
Love Is When You Meet A Man Who Doesn't Live With His Mother
Shelley Berman's Cleans & Dirtys
How To Be A Jewish Mother
How To Be An Italian
The Very Important Person Note Book
and many, many more

They are available wherever books are sold
or may be ordered directly from the publisher.
For a complete list, write:

Dept. TS-3
PRICE/STERN/SLOAN
Publishers, Inc.
410 North La Cienega Boulevard
Los Angeles, California 90048